# Life in the New American Nation™

# New Roads, Canals, and Railroads in Early-19th-Century America

## The Transportation Revolution

### Kurt Ray

rosen central
**Primary Source**™

The Rosen Publishing Group, Inc., New York

Published in 2004 by The Rosen Publishing Group, Inc.
29 East 21st Street, New York, NY 10010

**Library of Congress Cataloging-in-Publication Data**

Ray, Kurt.
New roads, canals, and railroads in early-19th-century America: the transportation revolution / by Kurt Ray.
    p. cm. — (Life in the new American nation)
Summary: Explores the beginnings of modern transportation in the nineteenth century, when the influx of immigrants required better roads, safe water routes, and railroads to be built across the United States. Includes bibliographical references and index.
ISBN 0-8239-4036-5 (lib. bdg.)
ISBN 0-8239-4254-6 (pbk. bdg.)
6-pack ISBN 0-8239-4267-8
1. Transportation—United States—History—19th century—Juvenile literature.
[1. Transportation—History—19th century.] I. Title. II. Series.
HE203.R39 2003
388'.0973'09034—dc21

2002156105

*Manufactured in the United States of America*

Cover (left): Drawing of the American explorer Daniel Boone by R. Pollard
Cover (right): Photo of the First Train in Sargent, Custer County, Nebraska

Photo Credits: cover (left and right), pp. 1, 5, 8 (bottom), 10, 18 (top), 20 (inset), 23 © Library of Congress; pp. 8 (top), 18 (bottom), 24, 26 © Hulton/Archive/Getty Images; p. 14 © Corbis; pp. 17, 20 © Bettmann/Corbis.

Designer: Nelson Sá; Editor: Eliza Berkowitz; Photo Researcher: Nelson Sá

# Contents

Introduction     4

**Chapter 1**    From Mountain Paths to Turnpikes    7

**Chapter 2**    West by Water    12

**Chapter 3**    The Riverboats    16

**Chapter 4**    The Mighty Railroads    22

Glossary    28

Web Sites    30

Primary Source Image List    30

Index    31

# Introduction

As America grew in the late 1700s, so did its need to move people and supplies from one place to another. Transportation was needed to help the economy. It was necessary in order to buy and sell goods. Transportation was also needed to help protect America's borders, by moving soldiers from place to place. The development of new methods of traveling and shipping became known as the Transportation Revolution.

After the Revolutionary War ended in 1783, many Americans began leaving the original thirteen colonies and moving west. Thousands of settlers left their homes in New England. Many others moved from the states of Maryland and Virginia. The settlers hoped to establish new lives in what was then known as the Northwest Territory. This area later became the states of Ohio, Indiana, and Illinois. As these settlers followed each other on foot, on horseback, or in covered wagons, a small network of roads developed.

Many settlers made their livings as farmers. They worked the land to feed their families. They raised sheep, cattle, and chickens. They also sold crops and livestock in other locations. More and more farmers

This painting by Junius Brutus Stearns depicts the life of George Washington, the farmer. Many settlers were farmers. They sold whatever goods they harvested to make money to support their families. This picture shows workers harvesting hay on Washington's farm.

needed to sell their goods beyond their small towns and farms. The demand for sturdy roads and safe water routes increased.

At the same time, many immigrants were moving to America. Immigrants are people who come from another country. America was seen as a place where everyone had a chance to make his or her dreams come true. Immigrants brought manpower, but they also brought skill and craftsmanship to America. Without their talent and strength, America could never have developed a network of canals, highways, and railroads as quickly as it did.

The Transportation Revolution included the construction of the first roads and turnpikes. It also included the pounding of spikes along railroad ties and building giant steamboats along the Mississippi River. The Transportation Revolution had a huge impact on American lives. As settlers moved farther and farther west, the need to ship goods to faraway places increased. New industries were created to support railroads, shipping companies, and road construction. In time, American transportation became a symbol of the great American spirit.

# From Mountain Paths to Turnpikes

## Chapter 1

Settlers moving west had to find a way through the mountains. Usually, this meant following trails used by animals, such as buffalo. The Cumberland Gap was a passage across the Appalachian Mountains that herds of buffalo followed for centuries. Settlers from Virginia, Kentucky, and Tennessee followed the gap during their journeys to the Ohio Valley.

Despite difficult journeys, American settlers continued heading west. They established towns in what are now Columbus, Ohio; Indianapolis, Indiana; St. Louis, Missouri, and many other places. The new lands were ideal for farming. The demand for better transportation increased.

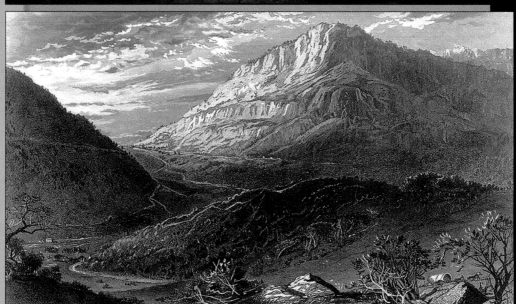

Many people traveled great distances as they settled in the West. Daniel Boone *(top)* led groups of settlers on the Wilderness Trail. The Cumberland Gap *(bottom)* was another popular way to travel west. Settlers followed the Cumberland Gap to get to the Ohio Valley.

Western farmers needed to ship their goods back to the East Coast to sell them. New roads had to be built.

One of the earliest roads built was the Lancaster Turnpike in western Pennsylvania. The Lancaster Turnpike was built in the style of a famous road in England. The road was constructed by laying down a base of large boulders. Smaller stones were piled on top of the boulders. Then pebbles and bits of crushed stone were put on top. The top layer was crushed together to make a solid surface. Like many modern roads, the Lancaster Turnpike was built with shoulders on both sides. Ditches were built on either side of the road to help water drain off the roadway.

## Daniel Boone and the Wilderness Trail

Daniel Boone was one of the earliest explorers of eastern Kentucky. In 1775, Boone became a paid guide for settlers moving west. He took them on the Wilderness Trail, which began in Kentucky, on the eastern side of the Appalachians. The trail eventually crossed the Cumberland Gap. For many years it was impossible for wagons to travel along the rough path. Most settlers traveled on foot or on horseback. The trail was dangerous, since it passed through Native American territories. Settlers who survived the dangerous journey reached Fort Boonesborough, established by Boone at the end of the Wilderness Trail.

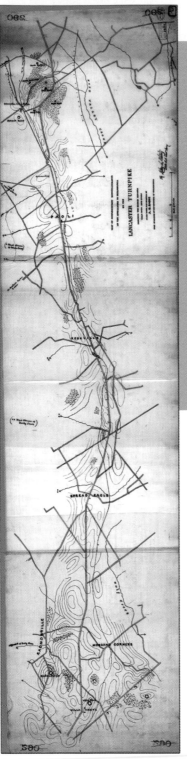

This map of the Lancaster Turnpike was created in 1863 by Henry L. Whiting. The Lancaster Turnpike was the first long-distance stone and gravel road in the country. The layers of crushed stone and gravel prevented the wheels of wagons from sinking through. The Lancaster Turnpike stretched from Philadelphia, Pennsylvania, to Lancaster, Pennsylvania, and opened the territory northwest of the Ohio River. The route of the turnpike was later replaced by a canal.

The Lancaster Turnpike took two years to build. It opened to travelers in 1794. The turnpike charged all who used it, even if they were traveling on foot! The road was a financial success. However, it was too expensive for many farmers to use. They began asking the government to build roads that everyone could use free of charge.

In 1811, the government began building the National Road. It was designed to connect the port of Baltimore, Maryland, with the Ohio River. Like the Lancaster Turnpike, the National Road (also called the Cumberland Road) was built with ditches on both sides. The road was very successful. Thousands of settlers used the road to move west in carts and wagons. Farmers in the West used the road to transport their goods to the East for sale. In 1833, Congress voted to extend the National Road even farther. Eventually the road stretched more than seven hundred miles, from Baltimore to Vandalia, Illinois.

# Chapter 2   West by Water

American rivers have been used for transportation for thousands of years. Native Americans built canoes from the bark of birch trees. They traveled in canoes along rivers and streams and crossed enormous lakes. Canoes allowed Native Americans to transport more supplies than they would be able to carry on foot. European explorers also used canoes in the early days of American exploration.

As settlers established farms and businesses in the Northwest Territory, they needed to ship goods on the rivers. Canoes were not big enough or sturdy enough for large, heavy loads. However, rivers could not always accommodate larger boats. River levels changed with the seasons. The natural twists and turns of a river could be difficult for boats to sail around. Waterfalls and shallows were dangerous for large boats. As a result, canals were built. Canals are man-made waterways.

The first canal in the United States was built in Massachusetts in 1793. The canal stretched a short distance, but it allowed boats to avoid rapids in the Connecticut River. In 1817, work began on the Erie Canal in New York State. The Erie Canal was built to connect Albany on the eastern side of New York with Buffalo on the western side, a distance of 350 miles. Since there would be no natural water flow within the canal, teams of horses would pull boats along the canal.

The development of canals allowed boats to be designed for different kinds of travel. Freighters were built for carrying large amounts of cargo. Packet ships were used for people who needed to travel quickly from one location to another. Line boats were designed for families that were relocating. Line boats carried many supplies, but they also had areas for families to sleep and eat. Line boats moved slowly because of their great weight, but they were still faster and safer than covered wagons.

Construction of canals was difficult and required a great deal of time. The Erie Canal was only four feet deep, but it was twenty-eight feet wide. Teams of men were paid to dig sections of the canal, usually one mile at a time. From dawn until dusk, the men dug the

The Erie Canal was opened on October 25, 1825. Boats used the canal to go from Buffalo to Albany, then traveled down the Hudson River to New York City. While people traveled west on this canal, farm produce was shipped east by the people in the west.

canal bed using shovels and picks. Stumps and boulders had to be removed. Teams of horses were used to pull away the largest objects. It took two years to complete the first fifteen miles of the Erie Canal.

Once the canal was dug, engineers had to construct a series of gates called locks. Locks were used to raise and lower boats over different levels of land and water. When a boat needed to get over a hill, it entered a section of canal between two locks. The lock was flooded with water until it reached the height of the water on the higher level. Then the lock was opened and the boat moved on to the next lock. The same process was used to lower a boat downhill.

The Erie Canal opened in 1825. The canal itself was 363 miles long. Boats traveling from Buffalo could enter the Hudson River at Albany. From there they could sail south to New York City. This made it possible for settlers in the West to ship goods many hundreds of miles to and from the East Coast.

# Chapter 3    The Riverboats

Canals were built where rivers and streams made boat travel impossible. Still, there were many rivers that flowed through the western regions that were large enough for boats of all sizes. The Missouri and Mississippi Rivers were the largest. As the nineteenth century progressed, both rivers became home to boats of many different styles.

Fur traders built round "bullboats" of willow branches and buffalo hides. These large boats could carry as much as six thousand pounds of fur or hides without sinking. However, bullboats took on water as they traveled. In order to stay afloat, they had to be unloaded and dried off every night.

This woodcut, created by Felix Octavius Carr Darley, shows how people traveled on rivers using flatboats. Often, farmers would use flatboats to carry their crops to market. Flatboats were easily created. They were made of pieces of wood, which could be sold as lumber after a farmer sold his crops.

Farmers often built flatboats to transport crops or livestock to faraway towns. Flatboats were large rafts that had enough room for a man or small family to live on during the journey. Flatboats were useful, but they were clumsy. They could carry goods downstream, but were very difficult to steer upstream. After selling their crops, farmers usually broke down the flatboats and sold them as lumber.

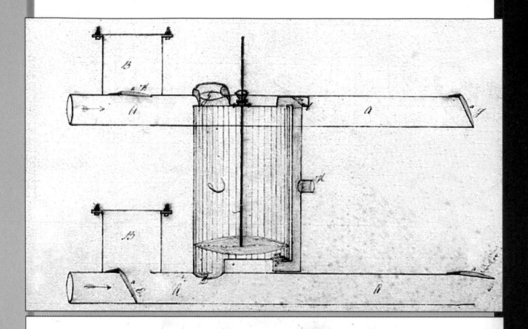

*Plan of M.ʳ Fitch's Steam Boat.*

John Fitch invented the first working steamboat in 1787. These are two of Fitch's sketches of his invention. Fitch's idea was to use steam to power a boat. The steam would move the oars. This would eliminate the need to have people using muscle power to move a boat and was a big improvement upon the boats that were used at the time.

Engineer John Fitch began work on a motorized boat in Pennsylvania in the 1780s. By 1790, Fitch created a paddleboat that traveled from Philadelphia, Pennsylvania, to Trenton, New Jersey, at a speed of eight miles an hour. Unfortunately, the boat could not carry enough paying passengers to make any money for Fitch.

Nearly twenty years later, the engineers Robert Fulton and Robert Livingston built steamboats that operated by using enormous paddle wheels that pushed the boats through the water. These boats used steam-powered engines and were called steamboats. Though the heavy engines were used successfully on the Hudson River, the boats failed to paddle upstream against the powerful current of the Mississippi River.

Finally, in 1816, engineer Henry Shreve created the first steamboat to successfully navigate the Mississippi River. The boat was named the *Washington*. The *Washington* was built much differently than the steamboats created by Fulton and Livingston. The *Washington's* engines were built on the deck of the ship instead of below it. The boat featured two separate

ROBERT FULTON'S CLERMONT-1809
COPYRIGHT 1909 BY IRVING UNDERHILL, NEW YORK

Robert Fulton *(inset)* helped create a type of steamboat that had steam-powered engines and paddle wheels that moved the boat along. This image of Fulton's boat, the *Clermont* *(above)*, was created in 1909, the same year it sailed on the Hudson River.

steam engines, one on each side, as well as a paddle wheel on each side. These features allowed the boat to float on top of the water, instead of sinking into it. The *Washington* was an instant success.

Steamboats like the *Washington* were built quickly in the years that followed. By 1859, there were more than one thousand steamboats being used on American rivers. Steamboats became a familiar part of American life. In addition to carrying cargo, steamboats became a favorite mode of transportation for passengers. Steamboat races were a common form of entertainment.

Most steamboats lasted fewer than five years. Though steamboats floated lightly on top of the water, the light lumber used to build them could easily catch fire. The large boilers used to power the paddle wheels could explode when overworked. During the Civil War, many steamboats were destroyed in battle.

## The First Cruise Ships

Many steamboats were constructed with first-class passengers in mind. Expensive furniture, fabrics, and stained glass were used to create guest rooms for people who could afford the luxury. Some steamboats included saloons, restaurants, and sleeping quarters. Others featured theatrical performances. These added attractions brought in a lot of money. Steamboat owners could make as much as $50,000 for a long voyage.

# Chapter 4

## The Mighty Railroads

As transportation improved during the 1800s, American needs kept growing. More people continued to move west. More goods needed to reach places that were farther away. Canals, steamboats, and new roads all helped. Still, nothing had as great an impact on American life as the construction of the railroads.

The earliest railroad in the United States was built in 1826. It was used to transport granite from a quarry to boats on the Neponset River in Massachusetts. As with canal boats, horses pulled the train cars forward. Once a steam engine was put to use, however, things began to change.

Between 1830 and 1835, nearly two thousand miles of railroad tracks were laid, most of them in the northeastern United States. By 1848, there were more than five thousand miles of tracks.

When gold was discovered in California in 1848, people rushed to the West to try and make money during what was called the gold rush. This handbill from 1849 advertises a steamship going directly to California so that passengers can take part in the search for gold.

Also in 1848, gold was discovered in California. The demand for access to the West was greater than ever.

This picture of workers laying down track for the Central Pacific Railroad is from 1868. While these workers were building railroad tracks to the east, the Union Pacific Railroad workers were laying tracks to the west. Many of the railroad workers were immigrants from other countries.

It took many years for Congress to agree on the path the railroad would follow from coast to coast. After ten years of surveying different routes, work began on the first transcontinental railroad in 1863. Beginning near Sacramento, California, workers from the Central Pacific Railroad laid tracks to the east. From Nebraska, workers from the Union Pacific Railroad laid tracks to the west.

Thousands of immigrants were allowed into the country to work on building the railroad. Most were from China and Ireland. Construction of the railroad was terribly hard work. Once a stretch of track was surveyed, workers had to clear trees, unload heavy tracks, and drive spikes into the hard ground. They worked in intense desert heat and brutal winter storms.

## Eating and Sleeping on the Rails

As with steamboats, there was a demand for luxury passenger compartments on trains. A former furniture builder named George Pullman spent much of his career perfecting passenger cars for the railroad. Pullman's luxury trains featured carpeting, mirrors, and dining cars. The sleeping cars had drop-down beds that could be used in the evening then put away during the day. Soon after, businessman Fred Harvey began opening restaurants and hotels at the larger train stations. Passengers could eat and drink at luxury restaurants while traveling in style.

Workers constructed bridges, blasted explosives through rock walls to create tunnels, and built wooden sheds to prevent snowdrifts from covering the tracks.

On May 10, 1859, the first transcontinental railroad was completed. The Central Pacific and Union Pacific Railroads joined together to form a stretch of track that went from coast to coast. The railroads continued to expand, and transportation in the United States was forever changed.

Finally, in 1869, the two stretches of railroad tracks met in Promontory, Utah. America now had a railroad that stretched from coast to coast. More transcontinental railroads followed. A northern route connected Portland, Oregon, to Lake Superior. A southern route connected San Francisco to New Orleans. The railroads changed the way Americans lived and did business.

The railroads marked the biggest advancement in transportation during the nineteenth century. Towns flourished near the railroad tracks, including Kansas City, Denver, Chicago, and Omaha. These cities became important industrial centers that contributed to the overall U.S. economy. They also became large urban centers, home to thousands of new American families each year.

By 1900, it was possible to cross the United States in less than a week. Trains were capable of pulling enormous shipments of goods from coast to coast. The government continued to assist new states in building safe and sturdy roadways. Large American rivers were home to thousands of ships transporting goods. In less than 125 years, the Transportation Revolution had changed the American way of life.

# Glossary

**canal (ka-NAL)** A man-made waterway built for boats.

**colonies (KAH-luh-neez)** Lands that are settled by citizens of another country, as the American colonies were originally settled by British citizens.

**downstream (DOWN-STREEM)** In the direction water is flowing naturally.

**granite (GRA-niht)** Hard, heavy, rock that is used for construction of buildings and monuments.

**immigrant (IH-muh-grint)** Someone who leaves his or her native country to live in another country.

**luxury (LUK-shuh-ree)** Something that adds pleasure or comfort.

**migrate (MY-grayt)** To move from one place to another in search of food or shelter.

**navigate (NA-vuh-gayt)** To steer a boat or ship, or to plan the path a boat will follow.

**obstacle (OB-stih-kul)** Something that gets in the way of progress.

**port (PORT)** A town or city where boats can load and unload goods.

**quarry (KWOR-ee)** A large hole, dug in the ground, from which stone is taken.

**settler (SET-ler)** Someone who is one of the first to live in a country or region.

**transcontinental (tranz-kon-tin-EN-tul)** Going from one side of a continent to the other.

**transportation (tranz-per-TAY-shun)** A way of moving something or someone.

# Web Sites

Due to the changing nature of Internet links, the Rosen Publishing Group, Inc., has developed an online list of Web sites related to the subject of this book. This site is updated regularly. Please use this link to access the list:

http://www.rosenlinks.com/lnan/nrcrenca

# Primary Source Image List

Page 1: Drawing on graphite paper. Created between 1861 and 1865. Housed in the Civil War Sketches at the New York Historical Society.

Page 5: Lithograph print painted by Junius Brutus Stearns and lithographed by Régnier. Created in 1853.

Page 8 (top): Painting done by George Caleb Bingham in 1851. Housed in Washington University Gallery of Art, St. Louis.

Page 8 (bottom): Engraving by Samuel Valentine Hunt in 1893 after a painting by Harry Fenn in 1872.

Page 10: Map by Henry L. Whiting. Created in 1863.

Page 17: A color woodcut painting done by Felix Octavius Carr Darley. Housed in Fine Arts Museums of San Francisco, California.

Page 18 (top): Sketch by John Fitch. Created in 1795.

Page 18 (bottom): Illustration by John Fitch. Created in 1787.

Page 20 (inset): Color drawing by W. Duke Sons & Co. Housed in the Rare Book, Manuscript, and Special Collections Library at Duke University.

Page 20: Illustration of the *Clermont* steamboat by Robert Fulton. Created around 1809 and engraved by Irving Underhill in 1909.

Page 23: Print by unknown artist. Created in 1849. Housed in the National Archives and Records Administration.

Page 24: Photograph taken in 1868. Housed in the Central Pacific Railroad Photographic History Museum.

Page 26: Photograph taken on May 10, 1869. Housed in the Central Pacific Railroad Photographic History Museum.

# Index

## A
Appalachian Mountains, 7, 9

## B
Boone, Daniel, 9
bullboats, 16

## C
California, discovery of gold in, 24
canals, 6, 13–15, 16, 22
Civil War, 21
Congress, 11, 25
Cumberland Gap, 7, 9

## E
Erie Canal, 13, 14–15

## F
farmers/farming, 5–6, 7, 9, 10–11, 17
Fitch, John, 19
flatboats, 17
Fort Boonesborough, 9
freighters, 13
Fulton, Robert, 19

## H
Harvey, Fred, 25
Hudson River, 15, 19

## I
Illinois, 4, 11
immigrants, 6, 25
Indiana, 4, 7

## K
Kentucky, 7, 9

## L
Lancaster Turnpike, 9, 10, 11
line boats, 13
Livingston, Robert, 19
locks, 15

## M
Maryland, 4, 11
Mississippi River, 6, 16, 19
Missouri River, 16

## N
National Road, 11
Native Americans, 9, 12
Northwest Territory, 4, 12

## O
Ohio, 4, 7
Ohio River, 11
Ohio Valley, 7

## P
packet ships, 13
paddleboat, 19
Pennsylvania, 9, 19
Pullman, George, 25

## R
railroads, 6, 22–27
Revolutionary War, 4

rivers, used for transportation, 12–13
roads, 4, 6, 9–11, 22, 27

**S**
Shreve, Henry, 19
steamboat racing, 21
steamboats, 6, 19–21, 22, 25

**T**
transcontinental railroad, 25–27

Transportation Revolution, 4, 6, 27

**V**
Virginia, 4, 7

**W**
*Washington*, 19–20
western expansion/movement, 4, 6, 7,
 9, 11, 22
Wilderness Trail, 9

## About the Author

Kurt Ray is a freelance author who has written many books for young adults. He lives in Bozeman, Montana, where he enjoys his passions for fly-fishing and the music of Artaud Filberto.